A Special Gift

For

Virginia O'Brien

From

Holly Peacemaker

Date

1-23-98

Message

Be back to work Soon ¨

Seasons

of

Happiness

~ Helen Steiner Rice ~

Fleming H. Revell
A Division of Baker Book House Co
Grand Rapids, Michigan 49516

SEASONS OF HAPPINESS

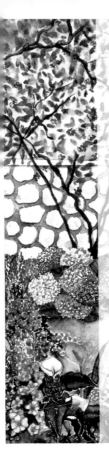

The Waking Earth

The waking earth in springtime
Reminds us it is true
That nothing really ever dies
That is not born anew.
So trust God's all-wise wisdom
And doubt the Father never,
For in His Heavenly Kingdom
There is nothing lost forever.

A Spring Awakening

Spring is God's way
of speaking to men
And saying, "Through Me
you will live again"
For death is a season
that man must pass through
And, just like the flowers,
God awakens him, too.

The Glory Of The Easter Story

In the glorious Easter story
A troubled world can find
Blessed reassurance
And enduring peace of mind.
For though we grow discouraged
In this world we're living in,
There is comfort just in knowing
God has triumphed over sin
For our Saviour's Resurrection
Was God's way of telling men
That in Christ we are eternal
And in Him we live again.
And to know life is unending
And God's love is endless, too,
Makes our daily tasks and burdens
So much easier to do.
For the blessed Easter story
Of Christ the living Lord,
Makes our earthly sorrow nothing
When compared with this reward.

An Easter Meditation

At this holy season
Give us quietness of mind,
Teach us to be patient
And help us to be kind,
Give us reassurance
That You are always near
To guide us and protect us
In this violent world of fear,
Help us all to realize
There is untold strength and power
When we seek the Lord and find Him
In our meditation hour.

Rejoice! It's Easter!

"Let not your heart be troubled"
Let not your soul be sad
Easter is a time of joy
When all hearts should be glad,
Glad to know that Jesus Christ
Made it possible for men
To have their sins forgiven
And, like Him, to live again.
So at this joyous season
May the wondrous Easter story
Renew our faith so we may be
Partakers of His Glory!

Mother's Day Is Remembrance Day

And we pause on the path of the year
    To pay honor and worshipful tribute
To the Mother our heart holds dear.
    For, whether here or in heaven,
Her love is our haven and guide,
    For always the memory of Mother
Is a beacon light shining inside.
    Time cannot destroy her memory
And years can never erase
    The tenderness and the beauty
Of the love in a Mother's face.
    And, when we think of our Mother,
We draw nearer to God above,
    For only God in His Greatness
Could fashion a Mother's love.

What Is A Mother?

It takes a Mother's Love
        to make a house a home,
A place to be remembered,
        no matter where we roam.
It takes a Mother's patience
        to bring a child up right,
And her courage and her cheerfulness
        to make a dark day bright.
It takes a Mother's thoughtfulness
        to mend the heart's deep "hurts",
And her skill and her endurance
        to mend little socks and shirts.
It takes a Mother's kindness
        to forgive us when we err,
To sympathize in trouble
        and bow her head in prayer.
It takes a Mother's wisdom
        to recognize our needs
And to give us reassurance
        by her loving words and deeds.

Motherhood

The dearest gifts that heaven holds,
The very finest, too,
Were made into one pattern
That was perfect, sweet, and true;
The angels smiled, well-pleased, and said:
"Compared to all the others,
This pattern is so wonderful
Let's use it just for Mothers!"
And through the years, a Mother
Has been all that's sweet and good
For there's a bit of God and love,
In all true Motherhood.

The Soul, Like Nature, Has Seasons, Too

When you feel cast down and despondently sad
And you long to be happy and carefree and glad,
Do you ask yourself, as I so often do,
Why must there be days that are cheerless and blue?
Why is the song silenced in the heart that was gay?
And then I ask God, "What makes life this way?"
And His explanation makes everything clear,
The soul has its seasons, the same as the year,
Man, too, must pass through life's autumn of death
And have his heart frozen by winter's cold breath.
But spring always comes with new life and birth
followed by summer to warm the soft earth.
And, oh, what a comfort to know there are reasons
That souls, like nature, must too have their seasons,
Bounteous seasons and barren ones, too,
Times for rejoicing and times to be blue.
For with nothing but "sameness" how dull life would be
For only life's challenge can set the soul free,
And it takes a mixture of both bitter and sweet
To season our lives and make them complete.

A Prayer For The Bride

Oh, God of love look down and bless
This radiant bride with happiness,
And fill her heart with "Love's Sweet Song"
Enough to last her whole life long
And give her patience when things disturb
So she can somehow gently curb
Hasty words in anger spoken,
Leaving two hearts sad and broken.
And give her guidance all through life
And keep her a loving, faithful wife.

Let Daily Prayers Dissolve Your Cares

We all have cares and problems
    we cannot solve alone
But if we go to God in prayer
    we are never on "our own".
And if we try to stand alone
    we are weak and we will fall,
For God is always greatest
    when we're helpless, lost, and small.
And no day is unmeetable
    if on rising our first thought
Is to thank God for the blessings
    that His loving care has brought.
For there can be no failures
    or hopeless, unsaved sinners
If we enlist the help of God
    who makes all losers winners.

So meet Him in the morning
and go with Him through the day
And thank Him for His guidance
each evening when you pray.
And if you follow faithfully
this daily way to pray
You will never in your lifetime
face another "hopeless day".
For like a soaring eagle
you too can rise above
The "storms of life" around you
on the wings of prayer and love.

With Faith In Each Other
And Faith In The Lord

With faith in each other
      and faith in the Lord
May your marriage be blessed
      with love's priceless reward,
For love that endures
      and makes life worth living
Is built on strong faith
      and unselfish giving.
So have faith, and the Lord
      will guide both of you through
The glorious new life
      that is waiting for you.

Another Anniversary!
Another Link Of Love!

It only seems like yesterday
That you were a radiant bride
With a proud and happy bridegroom
Standing at your side.
And looking back across the years
On a happy day like this
Brings many treasured memories
As you fondly reminisce.
And while you've had your arguments
And little "tiffs", its true,
And countless little problems
To vex and worry you.
For every "hurt and heartache"
And perhaps at times some "tears"
You've shared a world of happiness
Throughout your married years.
And looking back on this glad day
You both realize anew
That the sweetest words you ever said
Were just the words, "I do!"

God Bless Your Anniversary

This happy anniversary proves
a fact you can't disparage
It takes true love and faith and hope
to make a happy marriage.
And it takes a lot of praying
and a devoted man and wife
To keep God ever-present
in their home and in their life.
And you're a grand example
and an inspiration, too,
And every married couple
should be patterned after you.

A Graduate's Prayer

Father, I have knowledge,
    so will You show me now
How to use it wisely
    and find a way somehow
To make the world I live in
    a little better place,
And make life with its problems
    a bit easier to face.
Grant me faith and courage
    and put purpose in my days,
And show me how to serve Thee
    in the most effective ways
So all my education,
    my knowledge and my skill,
May find their true fulfillment
    as I learn to do Thy Will.
And may I ever be aware
    in everything I do
That knowledge comes from learning
    and wisdom comes from You.

Fathers Are Wonderful People

Fathers are wonderful people
      too little understood,
And we do not sing their praises
      as often as we should.
For, somehow, Father seems to be
      the man who pays the bills,
While Mother binds up little hurts
      and nurses all our ills.
And Father struggles daily
      to live up to "his image"
As protector and provider
      and "hero of the scrimmage".
And perhaps that is the reason
      we sometimes get the notion
That Fathers are not subject
      to the thing we call emotion.
But if you look inside Dad's heart,
      where no one else can see,
You'll find he's sentimental
      and as "soft" as he can be.

But he's so busy every day
        in the gruelling race of life,
He leaves the sentimental stuff
        to his partner and his wife.
But Fathers are just *wonderful*
        in a million different ways,
And they merit loving compliments
        and accolades of praise.
For the only reason Dad aspires
        to fortune and success
Is to make the family proud of him
        and to bring them happiness.
And like our Heavenly Father,
        he's a guardian and a guide,
Someone that we can count on
        to be always on our side.

A Prayer Of Thanks

Thank you, God, for the beauty
     around me everywhere,
The gentle rain and glistening dew,
     the sunshine and the air,
The joyous gift of feeling
     the soul's soft, whispering voice
That speaks to me from deep within
     and makes my heart rejoice.

To Know

To know beyond belief that someone cares and hears
    Our prayers provides security for the soul, peace
    Of mind, and joy of heart that no earthly trials,
    Tribulations, sickness, or sorrow can penetrate.
    For faith makes it wholly possible to quietly endure
    The violent world around us, for in God we are secure!

A Favorite Prayer

God, open my eyes so I may see
And feel Your presence close to me.
Give me strength for my stumbling feet
As I battle the crowd on life's busy street,
And widen the vision of my unseeing eyes
So in passing faces I'll recognize
Not just a stranger, unloved and unknown,
But a friend with a heart that is much like my own.
Give me perception to make me aware
That scattered profusely on life's thoroughfare
Are the best gifts of God that we daily pass by
As we look at the world with an unseeing eye.

The End Of The Road Is But A Bend In The Road

When we feel we have nothing left to give
And we are sure that the "song has ended"
When our day seems over and the shadows fall
And the darkness of night has descended,
Where can we go to find the strength
To valiantly keep on trying,
Where can we find the hand that will dry
The tears that the heart is crying?
There's but one place to go and that is to God
And, dropping all pretense and pride,
We can pour out our problems without restraint

And gain strength with Him at our side,
And together we stand at life's crossroads
And view what we think is the end,
But God has a much bigger vision
And He tells us it's only a bend.
For the road goes on and is smoother,
And the "pause in the song" is a "rest",
And the part that's unsung and unfinished
Is the sweetest and richest and best.
So rest and relax and grow stronger,
Let go and let God share your load,
Your work is not finished or ended,
You've just come to "a bend in the road".

Yesterday ... Today ... And Tomorrow!

Yesterday's dead
Tomorrow's unborn,
So there's nothing to fear
And nothing to mourn,
For all that is past
And all that has been
Can never return
To be lived once again.
And what lies ahead
Or the things that will be
Are still in God's hands
So it is not up to me
To live in the future
That is God's great unknown,
For the past and the present
God claims for His own.
So all I need do

Is to live for Today
And trust God to show me
The truth and the way.
For it's only the memory
Of things that have been
And expecting tomorrow
To bring trouble again
That fills my today,
Which God wants to bless,
With uncertain fears
And borrowed distress.
For all I need live for
Is this one little minute,
For life's here and now
And eternity's in it.

A Birthday Message For Someone
Who Will Always Be Young

Some folks grow older with birthdays, it's true,
But others grow nicer as years widen their view,
And a heart that is young lends an aura of grace
That rivals in beauty a young, pretty face.
For no one would notice a few little wrinkles
When a kind, loving heart fills the eyes full of twinkles.
So don't count your years by the birthdays you've had,
But by things you have done to make other folks glad!

A Birthday Meditation

God in His loving and all-wise way
Makes the heart that once was young and gay
Serene and more gentle and less restless, too,
Content to remember the joys it once knew.
And all that we sought on the pathway of pleasure
Becomes but a memory to cherish and treasure.
The fast pace grows slower and the spirit serene,
And the soul can envision what the eyes
have not seen.
And so while life's springtime is sweet to recall,
The autumn of life is the best time of all,
For our wild youthful yearnings all gradually cease
And God fills our days with beauty and peace!

Life's Golden Autumn

Birthdays come and birthdays go
        and with them comes the thought
Of all the happy memories
        that the passing years have brought
And looking back across the years
        it's a joy to reminisce,
For memory opens wide the door
        on a happy day like this,
And with a sweet nostalgia
        we longingly recall
The happy days of long ago
        that seem the best of all.
But time cannot be halted
        in its swift and endless flight
And age is sure to follow youth
        as day comes after night.

And once again it's proven
    that the restless brain of man
Is powerless to alter
    God's great unchanging plan.
But while our step grows slower
    and we grow more tired, too,
The soul goes soaring upward
    to realms untouched and new,
For growing older only means
    the spirit grows serene
And we behold things with our souls
    that our eyes have never seen.
And birthdays are but gateways
    to eternal life above
Where "God's children" live forever
    in the beauty of His love.

Growing Older Is Part Of God's Plan

You can't "hold back the dawn"
Or "stop the tides from flowing"
Or "keep a rose from withering"
Or "still a wind that's blowing".
And time cannot be halted
in its swift and endless flight
For age is sure to follow youth
like day comes after night.
For He who sets our span of years
and watches from above
Replaces youth and beauty
with peace and truth and love.
And then our souls are privileged
to see a "hidden treasure"
That in our youth escaped our eyes
in our pursuit of pleasure.
So birthdays are but blessings
that open up the way
To the everlasting beauty
of God's eternal day.

Slowing Down

My days are so crowded and my hours are
So few ... and I can no longer work fast
like I used to do ... but I know I must
learn to be satisfied ... that God has not
completely denied ... the joy of working at
a much slower pace ... for as long as He
gives me a little place ... to work with
Him in His vineyard of love ... and to know
that He's helping me from above ... gives
me strength to meet each day ... as I
travel along life's changing way!

The Autumn Of Life

What a wonderful time is life's autumn
      when the leaves of the trees are all gold,
When God fills each day, as He sends it,
      with memories, priceless and old ...
What a treasure house filled with rare jewels
      are the blessings of year upon year,
When life has been lived as you've lived it
      in a home where God's presence is dear ...
And may the deep meaning surrounding this day,
      like the "paintbrush" of God up above,
Touch your life with wonderful blessings
      and fill your heart brimful with love!

A Christmas Prayer

God, make us aware
that in Thy name
The Holy Christ Child
humbly came
To live on earth
and leave behind
New faith and hope
for all mankind.
And make us aware
that the Christmas story
Is everyone's promise
of eternal glory.

What Would We Face This Christmas Morn If Jesus Christ Had Not Been Born?

In this world of violence
    and hatred and greed
Where men lust for power
    and scorn those in need,
What could we hope for
    and where could we go
To find comfort and courage
    on this earth below
If in Bethlehem's manger
    Christ had not been born
Many centuries ago
    on that first Christmas morn ...
For life everlasting
    and eternal glory
Were promised to man
    in the Christmas Story!

The Miracle Of Christmas

The wonderment
        in a small child's eyes,
The ageless awe
        in the Christmas skies,
The nameless joy
        that fills the air,
The throngs that kneel
        in praise and prayer ...
These are the things
        that make us know
That men may come
        and men may go,
But none will
        ever find a way
To banish Christ
        from Christmas Day ...
For with each child
        there's born again
A mystery
        that baffles men.

"Behold, I Bring You Good Tidings Of Great Joy"

"Glad Tidings" herald the Christ Child's birth
"Joy to the World" and "Peace on Earth"
"Glory to God",
let all men rejoice
And hearken once more to the "Angel's Voice".

It matters not who or what you are,
All men can behold "the Christmas star"
For the star that shone is shining still
In the hearts of men
of peace and good will,
It offers the answer to every man's need,
Regardless of color or race or creed.

So, joining together in brotherly love,
Let us worship again our Father above,
And forgetting our own little
selfish desires
May we seek what "the star" of Christmas
inspires.

Each Christmas God Renews His Promise

Long, long ago in a land far away,
There came the dawn
of the first Christmas Day,
And each year we see that promise reborn
That God gave the world
on that first Christmas morn.
For the silent stars in the timeless skies
And the wonderment
in a small child's eyes,
The Christmas songs that carollers sing,
The tidings of joy
that the Christmas bells ring

Remind us again of that still, silent night
When the heavens shone
with a wondrous light,
And the angels sang of Peace on Earth
And told men of
The Christ Child's birth.
For Christmas is more than a beautiful story,
It's the promise of life
and eternal glory.

Christmas Is A Season For Giving

Christmas is a season
For gifts of every kind,
All the glittering, pretty things
That Christmas shoppers find,
Baubles, beads, and bangles
Of silver and of gold.
Anything and everything
That can be bought or sold
Is given at this season
To place beneath the tree
For Christmas is a special time
For giving lavishly.
But there's one rare and priceless gift
That can't be sold or bought,
It's something poor or rich can give
For it's a loving thought –
And loving thoughts are something
For which no one can pay
And only loving hearts can give
This priceless gift away.

A Prayer For Christmas

God give us eyes this Christmas
        to see the Christmas Star,
And give us ears to hear the song
        of angels from afar.
And, with our eyes and ears attuned
        for a message from above,
Let "Christmas Angels" speak to us
        of hope and faith and love.
Hope to light our pathway
        when the way ahead is dark,
Hope to sing through stormy days
        with the sweetness of the lark,
Faith to trust in things unseen
        and know beyond all seeing
That it is in our Father's love
        we live and have our being,
And *love* to break down barriers
        of color, race, and creed,
Love to see and understand
        and help all those in need.

Rejoice! It's Christmas!

May the holy remembrance
of the first Christmas Day
Be our reassurance
Christ is not far away.
For on Christmas He came
to walk here on earth,
So let us find joy
in the news of His birth.

And let us find comfort
and strength for each day
In knowing that Christ
walked this same earthly way.

So He knows all our needs
and He hears every prayer
And He keeps all "His children"
always safe in His care.
And whenever we're troubled
and lost in despair
We have but to seek Him
and ask Him in prayer
To guide and direct us
and help us to bear
Our sickness and sorrow,
our worry and care.
So once more at Christmas
let the whole world rejoice
In the knowledge He answers
every prayer that we voice.

A New Beginning

It doesn't take a new year
to begin our lives anew —
God grants us new beginnings
each day the whole year through,
So never be discouraged
for there comes daily to all men
The chance to make another start
and begin all over again!

A Pattern For The New Year

"Love one another as I have loved you"
May seem impossible to do
But if you will try to trust and believe,
Great are the joys that you will receive.
For love makes us patient, understanding, and kind,
And we judge with our heart and not with our mind.
For as soon as love enters the heart's opened door,
The faults we once saw are not there anymore,
And the things that seemed wrong begin to look right
When viewed in the softness of love's gentle light.
For love works in ways that are wondrous and strange
And there is nothing in life that love cannot change,
And all that God promised will someday come true
When you love one another the way He loved you.

Show Me The Way

God, help me in my own small way
To somehow do something each day
To show You that I love You best
And that my faith will stand each test.
And let me serve You every day
And feel You near me when I pray
Oh, hear my prayer, dear God above,
And make me worthy of Your love!